Hank Aaron

JACOB MARGOLIES

Hank Aaron
HOME RUN KING

Franklin Watts
New York   London   Toronto   Sydney
A First Book

Cover photograph copyright © UPI/Bettmann Newsphotos

Photographs copyright ©: Focus on Sports, Inc.: pp. 2, 10;
UPI/Bettmann Newsphotos: pp. 11, 17 bottom, 22 top, 27, 36 top,
51, 56; National Baseball Hall of Fame, Cooperstown, N.Y.:
pp. 15, 30, 34, 41; Leader-Telegram, Eau Claire, WI.: p. 17 top;
AP/Wide World Photos: pp. 19, 26, 32, 36 bottom, 38, 45, 47, 53;
Jacob Margolies: p. 22 bottom.

Library of Congress Cataloging-in-Publication Data

Margolies, Jacob.
Hank Aaron: Home run king / by Jacob Margolies.
p.   cm.—(A First book)
Includes bibliographical references (p.   ) and index.
Summary: A biography of the man who hit more home runs than anyone
else in baseball. Includes discussion of the racism and segregation
he faced during his career.
ISBN 0-531-20075-2
1. Aaron, Hank, 1934– —Juvenile literature.   2. Baseball
players—United States—Biography—Juvenile literature.   [1. Aaron,
Hank, 1934– .   2. Baseball players.   3. Afro-Americans—
Biography.]   I. Title.   II. Series.
GV865.A25M27   1992
796.357'092—dc20
[B]   91-29776   CIP   AC

Contents

Hank Aaron

INTRODUCING HANK AARON

*T*here are few things that are harder to do than to hit a baseball thrown by a major league pitcher. The batter stands alone in the batter's box at home plate. The pitcher, looking down from the mound, stands only 60 feet and 6 inches (18.4 m) away and sends the small, white hard ball flying toward the plate at a speed of 90 miles (145 km) per hour. The batter has only a split second to react. He must decide instantly whether the pitched ball will arrive over the plate. If the batter chooses to swing, he must be quick enough to whip the bat around from behind his body to meet the ball at the very instant that it reaches the plate.

Even if the batter manages to make contact with the ball, there are nine players, including the

(Above) Hank Aaron assumes his batting stance while awaiting the pitch. (Facing page, top) Another baseball great, Willie Mays, slides safely into home plate after his home run for the New York Giants. (Bottom) Hank Aaron is greeted by his teammates after making his 715th home run. This beat Babe Ruth's record of 714 home runs.

pitcher, positioned around the playing field. They are ready to catch or stop any ball that the batter might be skilled enough to hit. On a truly extraordinary occasion, a player may hit a ball so hard, so high, and so far that it travels over the heads of all the fielders and out of the ballpark. Such a tremendous blow, a home run, is the most exciting thing that can happen in a baseball game.

During his long career, one man hit more home runs than anyone else who ever played major league baseball. There have been players who received more attention, but nobody has ever been able to equal the amazing and glorious feats accomplished by this man. This is his story.

FROM MOBILE TO THE MAJORS

*H*ank Aaron learned how to play baseball under the hot summer sun of Alabama. Aaron's high school did not have a baseball team, but he played softball with his friends in Mobile, Alabama, where he grew up. One day in 1951 while Aaron was playing softball, a neighbor of his named Ed Scott asked him to play on Sundays for a local professional team called the Mobile Bears. At first Aaron's mother, Estelle, would not give him permission to play, but eventually Scott convinced her that playing for the Bears might be a good opportunity for her son.

Hank Aaron was just seventeen years old, but he quickly proved himself to be one of the best players on the Mobile Bears. Later that year the

Indianapolis Clowns came into town to play a game against the Bears. That visit would mark the beginning of Hank's long career.

The Clowns were one of the most famous black baseball teams in the United States. In 1951 blacks faced a great deal of racial discrimination in their daily lives. Baseball was no exception. In 1947 Jackie Robinson had joined the Brooklyn Dodgers and become the first black allowed to play major league baseball in the twentieth century. For Aaron and his friends, Jackie Robinson was a hero. Even by 1951, though, only a very few blacks had been given the chance to play baseball in the major leagues.

Since they had not been welcome in the majors, black baseball players had formed their own teams. For many years, these teams traveled all over the country playing each other. Until Jackie Robinson, many of the greatest baseball players of the time never got a chance to play in the major leagues because they were black. Eventually, as blacks gained greater opportunities, the all-black teams disappeared.

The Indianapolis Clowns were very impressed with Aaron. In fact, that next spring they offered him $200 a month to join the team. In 1952 that was a lot of money to a poor eighteen-year-old. Aaron was the third oldest in a family of eight chil-

The Homestead Grays, a black baseball
team before baseball was integrated

dren. The Aarons had their own house but it had no electricity. They used kerosene lamps instead of light bulbs. For a toilet, the family had built an outhouse in the backyard. Hank's father, Herbert, supported the family by working long hours at very low pay for a shipbuilding company in Alabama. Hank loved playing baseball and he decided to accept the offer from Indianapolis.

LEAVING HOME

Aaron left home with only two pairs of pants, two sandwiches in a brown bag, and $2 in his pocket and took the first train ride of his life to join the Indianapolis team. He was so scared that he nearly got off the train and returned home. He did not, and the Clowns soon had a new young star.

Aaron found that playing for the Clowns was not much fun. After a game the team usually traveled by bus all through the night to play the next day in another city. Besides having to sleep on the bus, the Clowns often had to play on fields that were in very bad condition.

Aaron, however, would not be with the Clowns for long. He was hitting so many home runs that baseball people began to take notice of him. A scout for the Milwaukee Braves, a major league team,

(Above) Hank Aaron (at far left in the second row) with the Eau Claire Bears, a minor league team. (Right) A very young Hank Aaron in his second year of professional baseball with the Sally League.

had spotted Aaron. The Braves bought Aaron's contract from the Indianapolis Clowns, and assigned him to join the Braves' minor league team in Eau Claire, Wisconsin.

Aaron, still only eighteen years old, was now in a strange city, and for the first time, he had white teammates. All of a sudden Hank began to miss his family and feel homesick. He decided to quit the Eau Claire team and return home. He packed his suitcase and called his family to tell them he was coming home. His older brother, Herbert Jr., got on the phone and told him that it would be a big mistake to give up on baseball. He convinced Hank to stay in Wisconsin. Aaron went on to have an excellent year. The next year, he was promoted to a higher-level minor league team in Jacksonville, Florida.

FACING RACISM

The Jacksonville team was in the Sally League. All the teams in this league were based in the South, and until that year no blacks had ever been allowed to play in the Sally League. Because state laws in the South kept blacks and whites from using the same facilities, Aaron and his two black teammates could not stay in the same hotels or eat

Jackie Robinson attempting to steal home plate.
Robinson was the first black player to play on
what had been an all-white team.

at the same restaurants as their white teammates when the team was on the road. Instead, the three stayed in private homes of local black families. In some cities, opposing teams' fans would insult Aaron and his black teammates. There were even a few instances when their lives were threatened. Somehow, Aaron was strong enough not to let any of this distract him. He had the highest batting average in the entire league, hitting .362, and was voted 1953's Most Valuable Player in the Sally League.

Hank Aaron was not yet twenty, but he had seen a lot in the two years since he left home. He had also become a very good baseball player. Aaron now hoped that he was ready to make the big leap to the majors.

THIS IS
BASEBALL

HOW IT STARTED

Before continuing Hank Aaron's story, let's take a closer look at the game of baseball.

Nobody knows for sure when the first game of baseball was played. Most people who have studied its history think that some of the first baseball games were played around the year 1845 in New York City and in New Jersey, across the Hudson River from New York. There is a game called rounders that has long been played by children in England. The object of rounders is for the batter to hit a ball thrown by a pitcher and then circle bases to score runs. Although the rules of rounders are quite different from those of baseball, it seems likely that baseball was originally based on the game of rounders.

21

RULES OF THE GAME

The best way to learn how to play baseball is to actually play the game with your friends. The rules sound complicated, but once you are on the ball field it all seems easy.

In a game, the two teams take turns at bat and in the field. The team at bat gets to make three outs before it has to take its turn in the field. When it takes the field, the other team gets to bat. When both teams have made three outs, the inning is over. Most major league games are nine innings long, with extra innings played if the score is tied.

The object of the team at bat is to score runs. A team scores a run each time one of its players safely circles the three bases and returns to home plate. The team that scores more runs in the game wins.

When a batter hits the ball, he runs to first base. The batter is out if a fielder catches the hit ball before it touches the ground, or if the team in

(Above) A lithograph by Currier & Ives showing baseball in its early days.
(Bottom) A neighborhood or Little League game is probably the best way to learn baseball.

the field can throw the ball to its fielder at first base and that fielder then touches first base before the batter gets there.

If the batter gets to first base, he may stay there and wait for the next batter to give him a chance to work his way around the bases toward home. Or, if he has hit the ball well past the fielders, he may try to continue advancing around the bases.

A batter gets a strike against him if he swings at the ball and misses, or if he hits the ball backwards or far enough off to the side to be outside the playing field. A ball hit outside the playing field is called a foul ball. A strike is also called if the pitcher throws the ball over the plate between the batter's knees and shoulders and the batter does not swing. If a player hits a foul ball when he has two strikes, it is not counted as a strike and the batter gets another chance. The batter at the plate is out if he gets three strikes.

If the pitcher does not throw the ball over the plate, the pitch is called a ball. If he throws four balls to a batter, the batter is allowed to advance to first base. This is called a walk.

These are some of the basic rules of baseball. There are many games that are variations of baseball. The most popular is softball. The main difference between playing softball and baseball is that in softball a larger and softer ball is used and the pitcher must throw the ball underhand.

BASEBALL IN THE UNITED STATES AND ABROAD

Baseball has become an international sport. It is extremely popular in Latin America—especially the Dominican Republic, Mexico, Cuba, Puerto Rico, and Venezuela—and in the Far East of Asia—Japan, South Korea, and Taiwan.

In the United States, the major leagues are the top level of professional baseball. They have been around since 1876. For many years the best team in baseball was the New York Yankees. They had the most famous home run hitter ever to play the game. His name was Babe Ruth. Ruth was a huge man. No other player could hit the ball as far as he did. During his career, starting in 1914 and continuing through the 1920s and 1930s, Ruth hit 714 home runs. Nobody else in the years that followed came close to hitting as many home runs. Sportswriters said that nobody would ever break Ruth's record.

When people thought of baseball, the first thing they thought of was Babe Ruth and the tremendous

(Facing page) A Cuban pitcher warms up
before the start of a game in Latin American
Stadium in Havana, Cuba. (Above) Babe Ruth
hits a fly ball in a game in 1930.

blasts that zoomed off his bat. He was an American hero.

In 1954, twenty-year-old Hank Aaron did not even think about challenging Ruth's record of 714 home runs. Aaron's only concern that spring was to make the Milwaukee Braves' team. Little did he know that before his playing days were finished, the names of Aaron and Ruth would be linked together forever.

THE MILWAUKEE YEARS

MAKING IT IN THE BIG LEAGUES

The Milwaukee Braves figured that Bobby Thomson would be their left fielder for the 1954 season. Hank Aaron and many other players in the Milwaukee minor league system had come up to practice with the Braves' regular players during spring training in Florida. But the Braves planned to send the young Aaron back to the minors for another year once the regular season began.

During an exhibition game that spring, Thomson hit a ball deep to left field. He turned first base, raced toward second, and slid into the base. At the end of the play, Thomson could not get up. His foot had gotten caught in the dirt, and he was badly injured. Thomson was carried off on a stretcher. Later, doctors discovered he had broken his leg. Now the Braves had no one to play left field.

The Milwaukee Braves in 1957 (Hank Aaron is
fifth from the right, in the top row).

During the rest of spring training, Aaron hit the ball hard and fielded well. In one game, he hit a home run so far that the ball landed in a trailer park way beyond the stadium. The Braves' manager, Charlie Grimm, was impressed. He decided that twenty-year-old Hank Aaron would be the Braves' left fielder for the 1954 season.

In his first year in the majors, Hank had a pretty good season for a rookie. His batting average was .280; he hit 13 home runs and drove in 69 runs. Aaron was disappointed with his performance, but he really shouldn't have been. He was now facing the best competition in the world. The pitchers in the majors threw the ball harder and more accurately than anyone Hank had faced in Eau Claire or Jacksonville. Nearly every player coming up to the majors needs time to adjust to the higher level of play, and Hank Aaron was no exception.

The season ended in an unfortunate way for Aaron. It was late September, and Hank was having a great game. He went 5 for 5—5 hits in 5 times at bat. On his final hit, Hank hit a ball past the outfielders. He raced toward third base for a triple, but as he slid into the base his foot got caught in the dirt, causing his right leg to crumple. Right away, Aaron knew that he was badly hurt. In fact,

Hank Aaron in his batting pose for
the Milwaukee Braves

he had broken his leg. It was strange. Aaron had gotten a chance to play that year because Bobby Thomson had broken his leg, and now Aaron's season was ending with a similar injury. Luckily, Aaron's leg healed well that winter and he was ready to play when the following season began.

Hank Aaron moved to right field in 1955, and that was the position he would play for most of the rest of his career in baseball. Although he is best known as a great home run hitter, Aaron was also a very good fielder. He had a strong throwing arm, and was quick to judge in what direction and how far a ball hit to his part of the outfield would travel.

At the same time that Aaron was starting his career, another great outfielder was beginning his days in the major leagues. He was Willie Mays. Mays, who had joined the New York Giants in 1951, was a great hitter and a spectacular fielder. He always seemed to be making diving catches, and he liked to catch the ball below the waist. The fans loved Mays's enthusiastic style of play.

Aaron's style of play was not as sensational, and because of this, for many years he did not receive the attention he deserved. In his quiet way, Aaron was as great a player as Mays, but it would take a long time before the sportswriters and fans would recognize this.

Willie Mays, center, another great outfielder and
a contemporary of Hank Aaron

By the end of the 1955 season, Aaron had become a star. He had hit 27 home runs and led the National League with the most doubles. As in 1954, the Braves were a good team, but they were still not good enough to challenge for the league championship. That would soon change.

GLORY YEARS

The 1956 Milwaukee Braves had some excellent ballplayers. Eddie Mathews and Joe Adcock were two big sluggers who could be counted on to hit lots of home runs and to drive in runs. Having a big hitter like Mathews next to him in the lineup helped Aaron as a hitter. If weaker hitters had followed Aaron at bat, then opposing pitchers, fearful of Hank's power, might have been tempted to walk him. Then they could have faced the weaker batter. But with Mathews and Adcock in the lineup, they could not pitch around Aaron and were forced to throw strikes to him.

The Braves also had two of the best and craftiest pitchers in baseball in Lew Burdette and Warren Spahn. Spahn won more games in his career than any other left-handed pitcher in the history of baseball. He had a whole collection of great pitches. He threw an excellent fastball. His curve-

(Above) Hank Aaron, Joe Adcock,
and Eddie Mathews—three
reasons the Milwaukee Braves
were so successful.
(Right) Warren Spahn winds up
to throw one of his great pitches.

ball broke over the plate just as it arrived there, and his slider dipped down just as the batter began to swing at it. His change-up looked so much like a fastball to hitters that they swung at it before it reached the plate. But the pitch was actually traveling at a slower speed. And Spahn never seemed to throw any ball down the middle of the plate, where it was easiest to hit.

Led by these players, the Braves were in first place in the National League race for most of the year. With three games left in the season, the Braves led the Brooklyn Dodgers by one game. A few years later, the Dodgers moved to Los Angeles and became the team now known as the Los Angeles Dodgers.

The Braves' final three games in 1956 were against the St. Louis Cardinals. If the Braves could win two of those games, they would be the National League champions. They lost the first game to the Cardinals, 5 to 4. The next day, Spahn pitched a great game, but the Braves could not hit the St. Louis pitcher. St. Louis won the game, 2 to 1, and the Dodgers beat the Braves for the 1956 National League pennant.

It had been another excellent season for Hank Aaron. He was the National League batting champion with the highest average in the National

(Above) Hank Aaron is presented with a silver bat and the John Hillerich memorial award from National League president Warren Giles. Aaron received the honor for being batting champion of 1956 with a .328 average. (Left) Hank Aaron is carried from the field in triumph after his home run in the eleventh inning won the National League pennant for the Milwaukee Braves in 1957.

League, but he was upset with the way the season had ended. Hank was determined that 1957 would be different for the Braves.

The Braves started 1957 winning nine of their first ten games. For Hank Aaron it was a season he would never forget. He was hitting home runs, and driving in runs as he never had before. For a while, Aaron even played center field when the Braves regular center fielder, Billy Bruton, was injured. Near the end of the season, the Braves were challenged by the St. Louis Cardinals, the same team that had beaten them twice at the end of the previous season to deny them the National League championship.

On the night of September 23, the Braves faced off against the Cardinals. If the Braves won, they would be National League champs for 1957. The fans at Milwaukee's County Stadium had packed the stands in the hope of seeing their team win. At the end of nine innings it was 2 to 2, and the game went into extra innings. In the eleventh inning, with a runner on second base, Hank came up to the plate and faced the Cardinal pitcher, Billy Moffitt. Aaron saw a pitch he liked, timed his swing perfectly, and hit the pitch. The ball traveled, and traveled out of the ballpark. It was a home run, the game was over, and the Braves were the 1957

National League champs. The Braves' players carried Aaron off the field in celebration. Although he would hit hundreds more home runs over the years, Hank Aaron would often say that for him this one was the most memorable in his long career.

It had been a terrific season, and it was not over yet. Aaron had hit 44 home runs and driven in 132 runs in the regular season, and was voted the National League's Most Valuable Player. Now the Braves would play the American League winners, the New York Yankees, in the World Series. The Yankees seemed to be in the World Series nearly every year in those days. They had great players like Mickey Mantle and Elston Howard. Most people thought the Yankees would win it all. After six games, the Series was tied at three games each. In the seventh and final game, Lew Burdette shut out the Yankees, 5 to 0, and the Braves were world champions.

Aaron had played terrifically in the World Series, hitting three home runs against the Yankees. Although he could not have guessed it then, 1957

Hank Aaron forced out at second base in the 1957 World Series

40

would be the only time in his long career that Hank Aaron would get to play on a World Series winning team.

AARON SHINES, BUT THE BRAVES START A SLOW DECLINE

The Braves had excellent teams again in 1958 and 1959. In 1958 they returned to the World Series and faced off once more against the Yankees. As in 1957, the Series went to a seventh and deciding game, but this time the Yankees won, 6 to 2.

The following year was more disappointing. Hank had a great season, hitting 39 homers, with a .355 batting average. The Braves ended the season tied with the Los Angeles Dodgers and faced them in a three-game playoff. The Braves lost the first game but they still figured they could beat the Dodgers to win the National League championship. In the second game, the Braves looked set to win as they led, 5 to 2, going into the ninth inning. Then the Dodgers staged a comeback and tied the game. The game went into extra innings, and Los Angeles won it in the twelfth. The Dodgers were the 1959 league champions. Aaron and his teammates were shocked. After the game nobody felt like talking in the Braves' dressing room.

From 1956 to 1959 the Braves had been one of the best teams in baseball. They had won the National League championship in 1957 and 1958, and come very close to winning in 1956 and 1959. In the 1960s, however, the Braves team was not as successful. Milwaukee made some bad trades, and some of the older players retired. Still, Hank Aaron kept hitting home runs. From 1957 through 1965, he hit at least 30 home runs every year except one.

The great pitcher Robin Roberts once complained, "How can you fool Aaron? He falls asleep between pitches." Actually Aaron always concentrated, and never let anything distract him when he went to the plate. He was so focused and relaxed in the batter's box that it sometimes seemed that he was in another world. Pitchers facing Aaron learned very quickly that he was not asleep at the plate.

THE LONG CHASE

ATLANTA

After the 1965 season, the Braves team moved to Atlanta. Hank Aaron was heading down South, back to the part of the country where he had grown up. Until the Braves' move, there had never been a major league team in the heart of the South. Now fans from that region of the country would have a team that they could root for as their own. Aaron was excited about moving to Atlanta, but he was also sad to leave Milwaukee after eleven years there. Aaron and his wife and four children had made many friends in Milwaukee; now they would need to start over in a new city.

Hank kept on hitting home runs. During the Braves' first year in Atlanta, he hit 44 homers. The next year he hit 39. Because the Braves team was

More than 37,000 fans jammed Atlanta's
new stadium to see the Milwaukee Braves
defeat the Detroit Tigers in 1965.

not very good, it did not get a lot of newspaper and television coverage, so Aaron's accomplishments were not given much attention. As his home run totals continued to rise, however, it became impossible to ignore his hitting feats.

On July 14, 1968, Aaron stepped up to the plate and faced Mike McCormick of the San Francisco Giants. The previous year McCormick had been selected as the best pitcher in the National League. Aaron saw a pitch he liked and drove the ball out of the park. It was the 500th home run of his career. Only a handful of players in the history of baseball had ever hit 500 home runs. Although most people thought that it was impossible, a few people began to wonder whether Aaron might someday challenge Babe Ruth's incredible record of 714 home runs.

Hank Aaron's last chance to play for a championship team came in 1969. New teams had been added to both the National and American Leagues, and the leagues had been broken up into eastern and western divisions. Even though they were on the eastern side of the United States, the Atlanta Braves were placed in the National League Western Division.

Led by Aaron, the Braves won the 1969 Western Division title and then faced the 1969 National

Hank Aaron as he slams his 500th home
run in Atlanta. He became the eighth man
in history to hit 500 homers.

League East champions, the New York Mets. The Mets beat the Braves easily, and Atlanta's season was over. But it had been another great year for Aaron at the plate. He had hit 44 home runs, and earned a .300 batting average.

Age did not seem to be slowing down Hank Aaron. More people began to wonder if Aaron could match Ruth's home run record. Sportswriters around the country started to follow Aaron more closely. Most people were interested in seeing Hank hit home runs, but he was setting other records too.

In 1970, Aaron got a base hit in a game against the Cincinnati Reds. It was the 3,000th hit of his career. Only eight players had ever made 3,000 hits in the history of modern baseball. Even Babe Ruth had not done it. Aaron said later that having over 3,000 hits meant more to him than his home run record because it showed his consistently good performance over the years.

Still, Aaron continued his home run assault. He hit 47 home runs in 1971, more than in any other year in his career. The records continued to fall. When he started the 1973 season, Aaron had 673 home runs. Over the next two years every move Hank made would be followed and commented on by reporters from all over the world. It should have been the happiest and most exciting period of Aaron's career. Instead, it became a very difficult time. He would not be able to enjoy his pursuit of Ruth's home run record until his playing days were over.

CLOSING IN

Older fans saw Babe Ruth as a great hero. There were many stories about Ruth's huge appetite for food, his loud boasts, and his powerful home runs. Most baseball fans had thought Ruth's home run record would stand forever.

Aaron's quiet, hardworking style was very different from Ruth's. Some people were not happy that Aaron might surpass the magnificent Babe Ruth. There were some biased fans who did not like the idea of a black man holding the record as baseball's all-time home run king.

As the 1973 season got under way, Aaron's life underwent a dramatic change. After every game, dozens of reporters crowded around him asking him endless questions. Aaron received nearly a million letters that year in the mail. Most of the letters encouraged him in his pursuit of Ruth's record, but some were very nasty. Aaron even began receiving threats on his life.

In order to ensure his safety, Aaron sometimes had to stay at a separate hotel from his teammates when the Braves traveled. He could not eat meals with the other Braves. Atlanta even had a security man assigned to protect Hank at all times. Aaron was shocked and upset by the threats against him, but he did not let it affect his performance. In fact, all the commotion made him even more determined to succeed.

Aaron would need 41 home runs during the 1973 season to tie Ruth's record of 714 homers. Even at the age of thirty-nine, he was still proving himself to be one of the best home run hitters in the game. Near the end of the year, fans flocked to see Aaron wherever the Braves were playing. He ended the season with 40 home runs. That left him with 713 lifetime home runs, just two short of breaking Ruth's record. The record would now have to wait for the 1974 season.

HOME RUN KING

It was Opening Day 1974, and the Braves were in Cincinnati. This year Aaron wasted no time. He hit home run 714 in Atlanta's first game of the year. Now with just one more home run Aaron would make baseball history.

Less than a week later, the Braves were at home facing the Los Angeles Dodgers. It was Atlanta's first game of the year at Atlanta Stadium. Over 50,000 fans filled the stands hoping to see history

Hank Aaron runs toward his wife
after his 714th home run.

made. Before the game, the mayor of Atlanta and the governor of Georgia gave speeches. There was even a fireworks display.

Hank Aaron was eager to finally hit home run number 715. The first time he got up to bat he did not get a chance; the Los Angeles pitcher, Al Downing, walked him. The fans booed. They wanted Downing to throw a pitch into the strike zone that Aaron would have a chance to hit. In the fourth inning Aaron came up again. This time Downing threw a high fastball, and Aaron hit the ball hard to left field. The Dodger left fielder and center fielder both ran back toward the left field fence, but the ball kept traveling. It traveled right over the fence. Aaron had hit home run number 715! His teammates raised him on their shoulders, and Aaron's parents, Herbert and Estelle, came out of the stands to celebrate with him. Television programs all over the United States were interrupted to break the news. Hank Aaron was the new all-time home run king. He had done it. Aaron was happy and relieved. Finally, it was over.

FINISHING UP

Aaron's career was not finished. He completed the season with the Atlanta Braves. At the end of the year, he signed a contract to play with

Hank Aaron beams as he holds a Milwaukee Brewers jersey against his chest.

the Milwaukee Brewers in the American League. He would return to Milwaukee, where he had had his happiest years as a baseball player. The switch to the American League was difficult for Aaron. He was over forty, and suddenly he had to learn about an entirely new set of pitchers and ballparks. Hank played two years in Milwaukee, 1975 and 1976, before retiring.

When he finally ended his playing days, Hank Aaron could point to a collection of marvelous records. In addition to hitting 755 home runs, he had more runs batted in and more extra-base hits than any player in the history of major league baseball. Although for most of his career he did not get the credit he deserved, by the time he retired everybody recognized Hank Aaron as one of the greatest baseball players of all time.

AFTER THE RECORD

*H*ank Aaron was elected to the Baseball Hall of Fame as one of the sport's all-time greatest players in 1982. Although Aaron's playing days are over, he is still very involved with baseball as a top-level executive. As the executive vice president for player personnel of the Atlanta Braves until 1990, Aaron was in charge of the Braves' minor league teams. He talked to scouts and reviewed all the players in the Atlanta system. He was always on the lookout for a young player on a minor league team in a place like Eau Claire or Jacksonville who might turn into another Hank Aaron. Aaron is still with the Braves, but he recently gave up his responsibility for the Braves' minor league teams.

Aaron has also been very active in speaking

Hank Aaron at a press conference after he was
elected to the Baseball Hall of Fame

out on the need for the major leagues to hire more black managers, coaches, and front-office executives. Baseball is a game Hank Aaron has loved and cared about for over forty years, and it remains to this day a very big part of his life.

Glossary

Batting average—a hitter's batting average is determined by dividing the number of his hits by the number of times he officially went to bat (known as "at bats"). For example, a player who had 3 hits in 10 at bats would have a batting average of .300 (3 ÷ 10 = .300). If a batter walks or sacrifices (makes an out while advancing a runner already on base), his time at the plate is not counted as an official at bat.

Runs batted in, or RBIs—a batter is credited with a run batted in when through his at bat he causes a runner on base to score a run. For example, if there are base runners on first and second and the batter hits a triple, both runners on base would then score runs and the batter would be credited with two runs batted in.

Shutout—a game in which one team fails to score is a shutout. The team that fails to score has been shut out by the winning team.

Slide—when a base runner dives, either feet first or head first, into a base to elude the fielder's attempt to tag him with the ball, this is known as a slide.

Slugger—a batter who has great power and hits lots of home runs is called a slugger.

For Further Reading

Aaseng, Nathan. *Baseball's Greatest Teams.* Minneapolis, MN: Lerner, 1985.

Epstein, Sam and Beryl. *Baseball's Gallant Fighter.* Dallas, TX: Garrard, 1974. A biography of Jackie Robinson, who broke the color barrier and integrated baseball.

Humphrey, Kathryn. *Satchel Paige.* New York: Franklin Watts, 1988. A biography of Paige, a great pitcher who played in the Negro Leagues for many years when baseball was still segregated.

Van Riper, Guernsy. *Babe Ruth: Baseball Boy.* New York: Macmillan, 1959.

Walker, Henry. *Illustrated Baseball Dictionary for Young People.* Illustrated by Leonard Kessler. Jupiter, FL: Treehouse, 1978.

Index